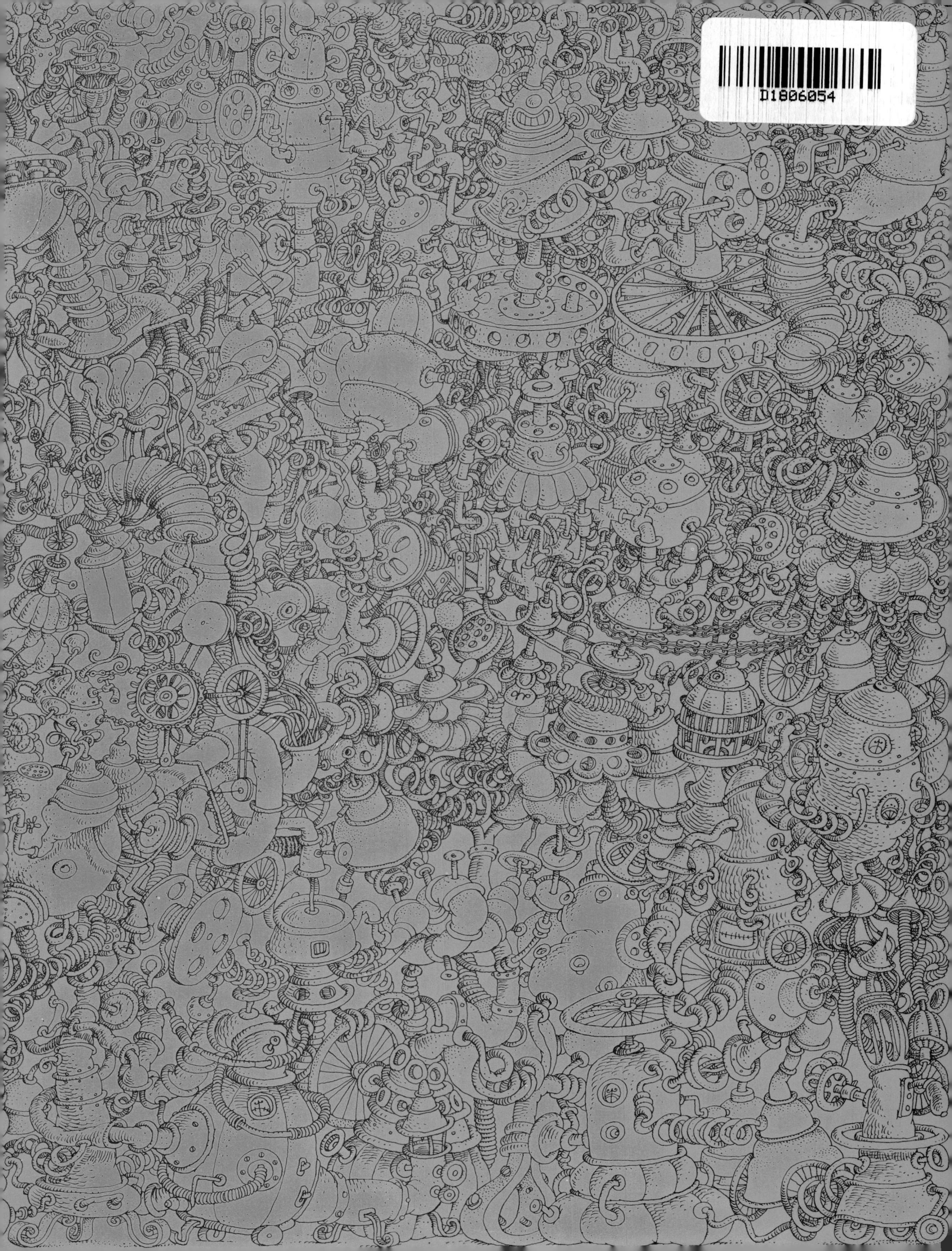

A OSKI

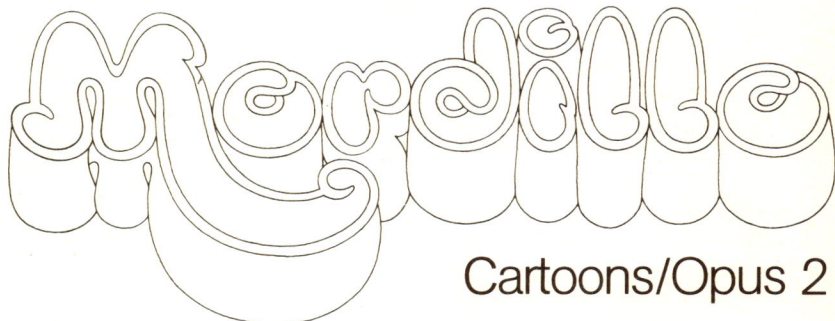

Cartoons/Opus 2

Cartoons/Opus 2

Hutchinson & Co. (Publishers) Ltd
An imprint of the Hutchinson Publishing Group
17-21 Conway Street, London W1P 5HL

Hutchinson Group (Australia) Pty Ltd
30-32 Cremorne Street, Richmond South, Victoria 3121
PO Box 151, Broadway, New South Wales 2007

Hutchinson Group (NZ) Ltd
32-34 View Road, PO Box 40-086 Glenfield, Auckland 10

Hutchinson Group (SA) Pty Ltd
PO Box 337, Bergvlei 2012, South Africa

First published in Great Britain 1982
© 1978 Guillermo Mordillo. All rights held by
Friedrich W. Heye Verlag GmbH, Munchen/Hamburg
Printed by Librex, Milan, Italy
ISBN 0 09 146940 6

Where words fail, pictures speak clearly – and vice versa

Looking at Mordillo's drawings is like watching a film whose sudden twists and turns are constantly startling. Each picture follows hot-foot upon its predecessor, striking the eye and the subconscious with the clarity of a magic lantern. The unexpected conforms to the rationale of the Absurd. Mordillo is one of the really great masters of 'black comedy', masters like Walt Disney and Steinberg who with a few strokes of the pen have created a world blending surprise and fantasy.

Humour is sometimes cruel: at a street corner a kindly fellow comes across a man winding up a winch on the wall. Our bemused hero walks on without suspecting that at the end of the street a huge mallet waits to knock him down. This implement is actually powered by the winch wound up by the man on the first street corner.

The drawings ramble face to face with the Absurd and the reader pursues them dreamily and in awe. Mordillo's is an entirely visual art – the unexpected

 hits one between the eyes: a man runs towards a round object on which a plump, pinkish ostrich egg is lying. The whole thing resembles a gigantic breast. Suddenly the man stops dead in his tracks – the shape has cracked open to reveal shark-like razor-sharp fangs.

Humour is sometimes wild too: occasionally there is a parallel between the art of cartoons and the art of mime where the plot constantly produces more startling revelations. A lofty wooden fence conceals a running man – a head and shoulders project over the top of the fence, the feet can be seen underneath. He appears to be a giant, but between head and feet, where the fence is not solid but only boarded together by a couple of struts we discover two tiny men, one running on the upper plank, one on the lower. These visual jokes develop like the films of Charlie Chaplin, Buster Keaton, Laurel and Hardy and the Marx Brothers. In many instances the comic illusion strikes up an affinity with

 the art of mime by direct allusion to the medium where action and gesture combine to form a parable. Mordillo's mastery stems from the grace of his drawings and from his sensitive approach. His line drawings, sometimes bold, sometimes delicate, are amazingly balanced; his cheerful water-colours reveal a painter of considerable dramatic force.

Mordillo once said that he believed in man's future in spite of everything. This attitude is the heritage of the wit of Cervantes, whose hero Don Quixote jousted with windmills. The humorist, as we love him in Mordillo, confidently expresses his own powers of emotional feeling and wit.

Emotionally and visually, Mordillo reveals himself as intrinsically a poet. His pathetic, grotesque or ridiculous figures express a transitory yet lyrical heroism. They present themselves to us as testimony to the acknowledged cruelty of human stupidity, the root cause of all life's haps and mishaps. In doing this,

 however, Mordillo betrays his faith in man's essential nobility. So much tenderness and love is hidden in the colourful book of cartoons that we begin to dream and to hope in spite of the inexorability of Fate which hangs over our heads like the relentless seal of eternity.

MARCEL MARCEAU

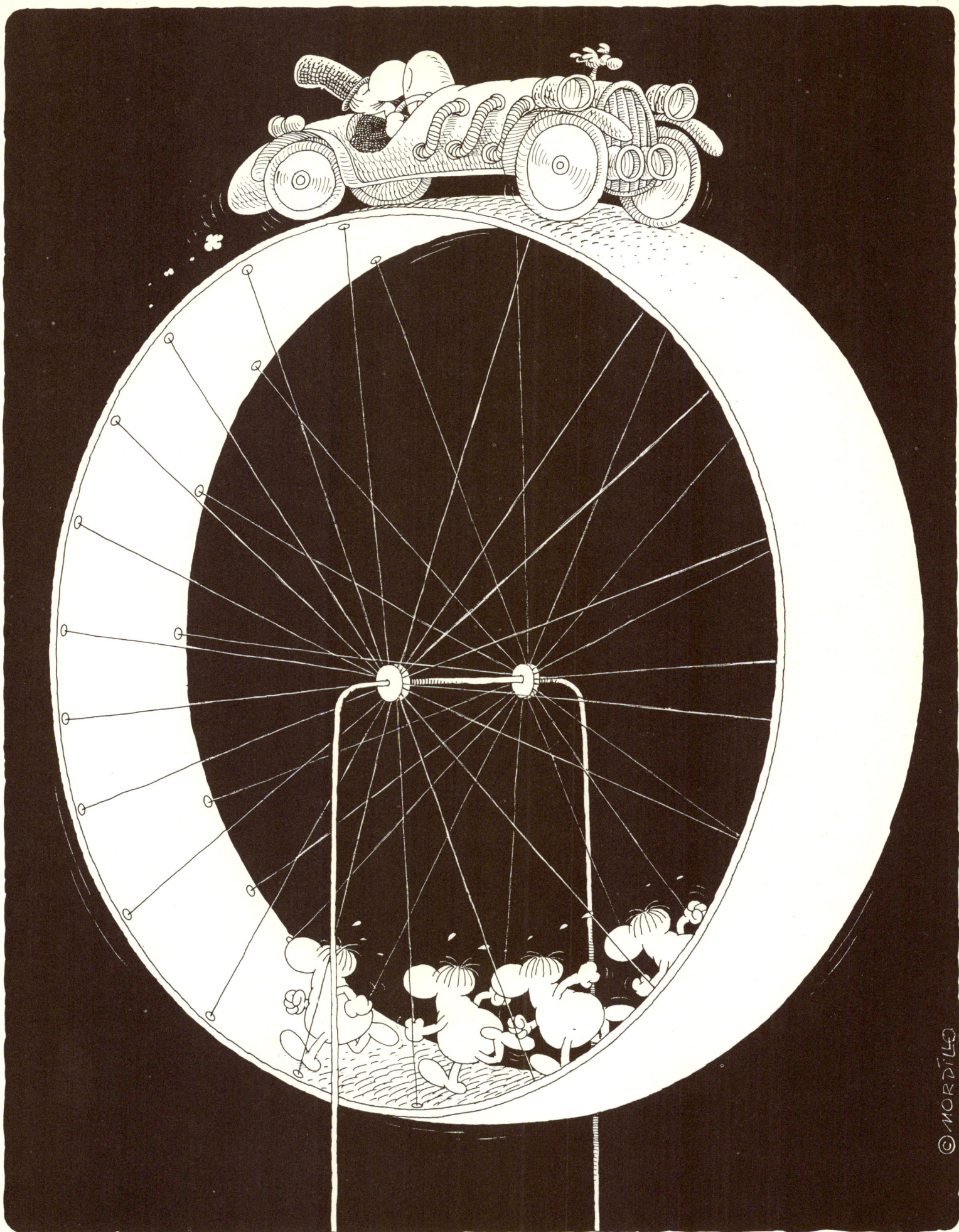

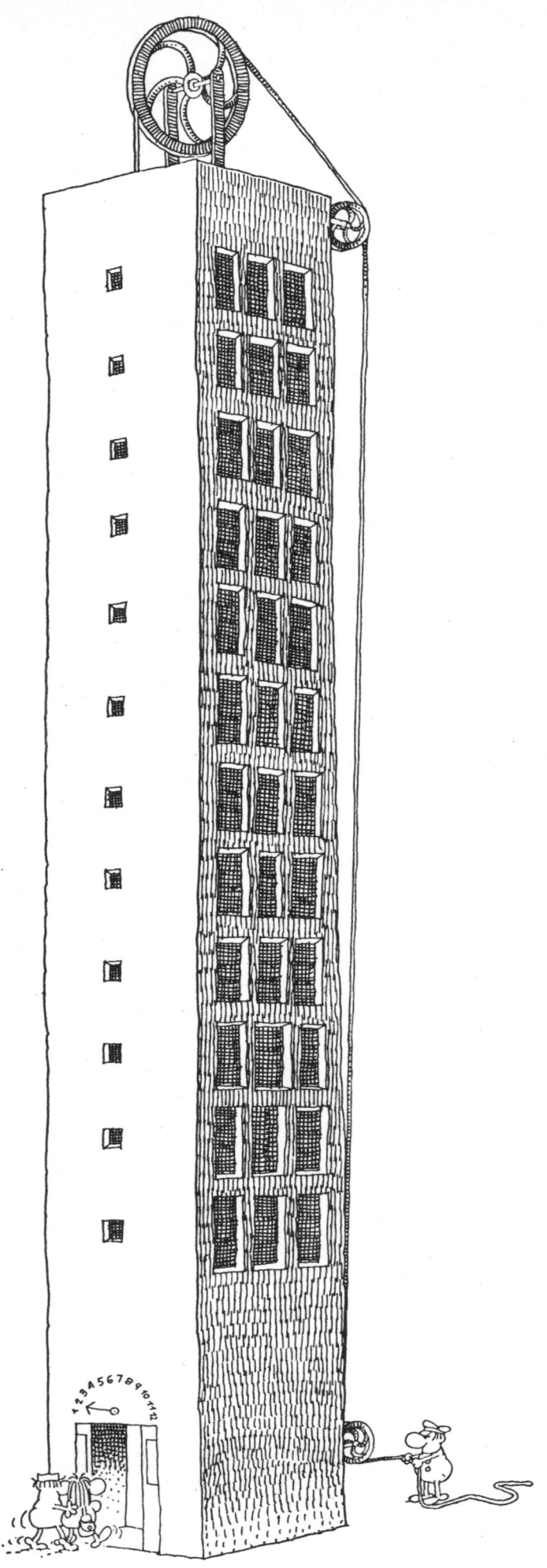

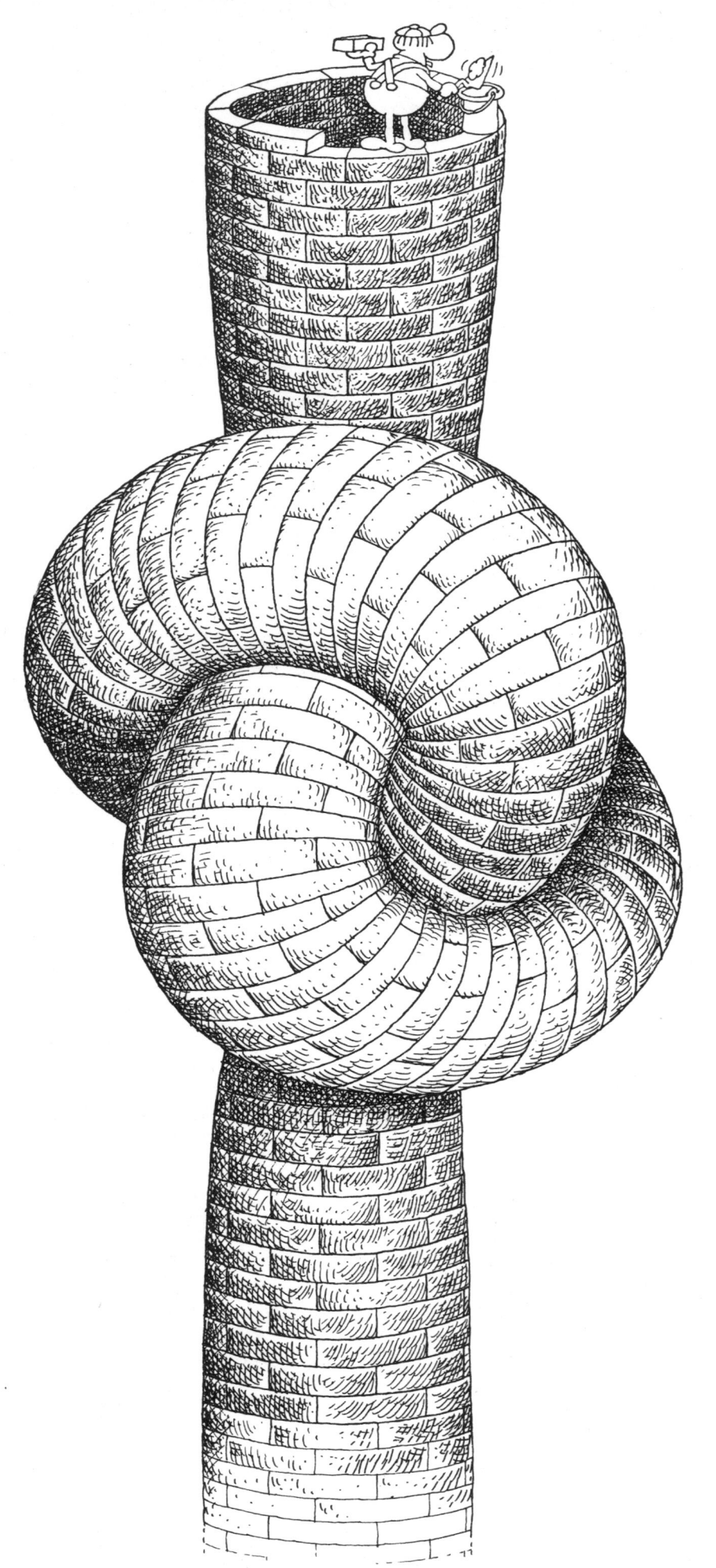

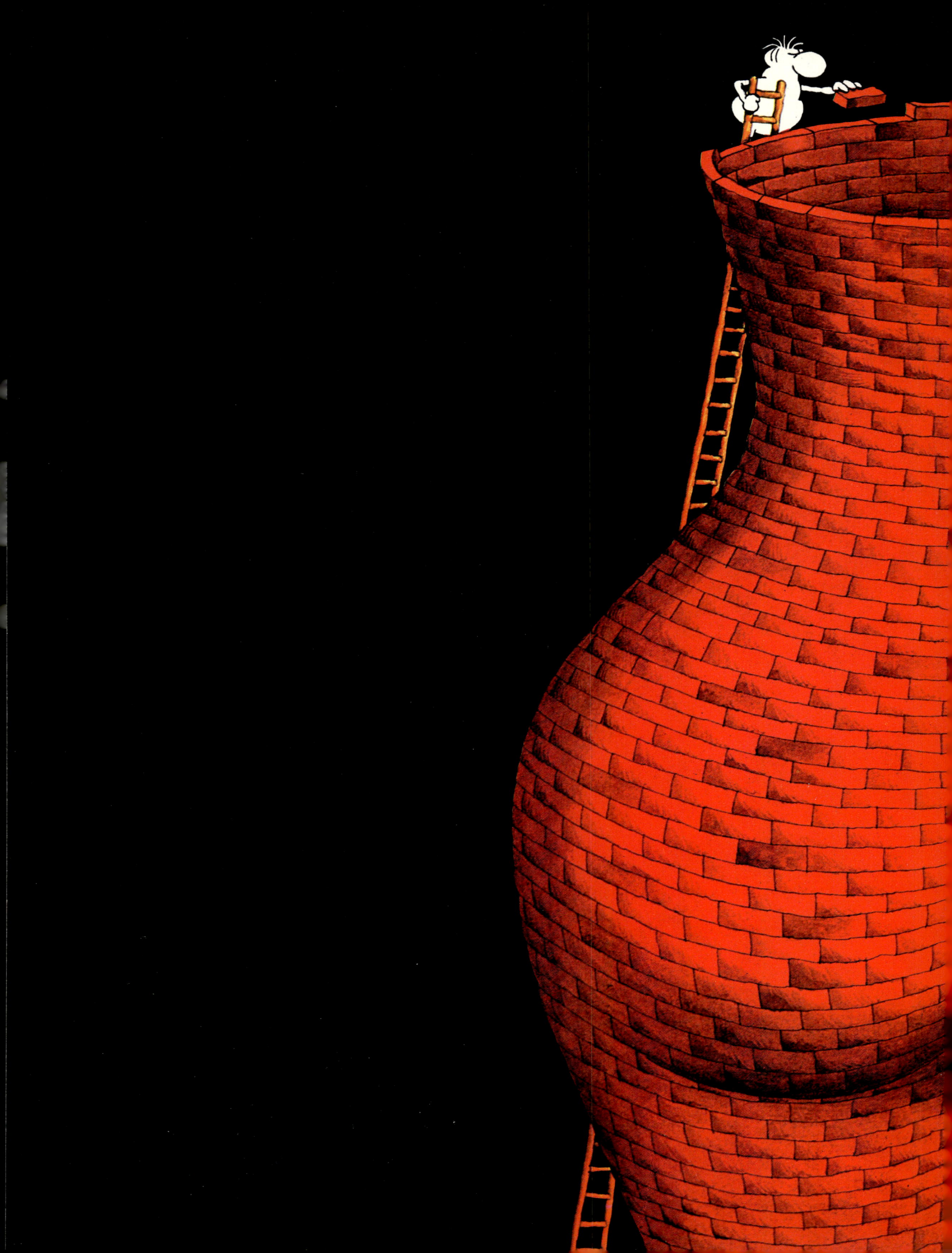

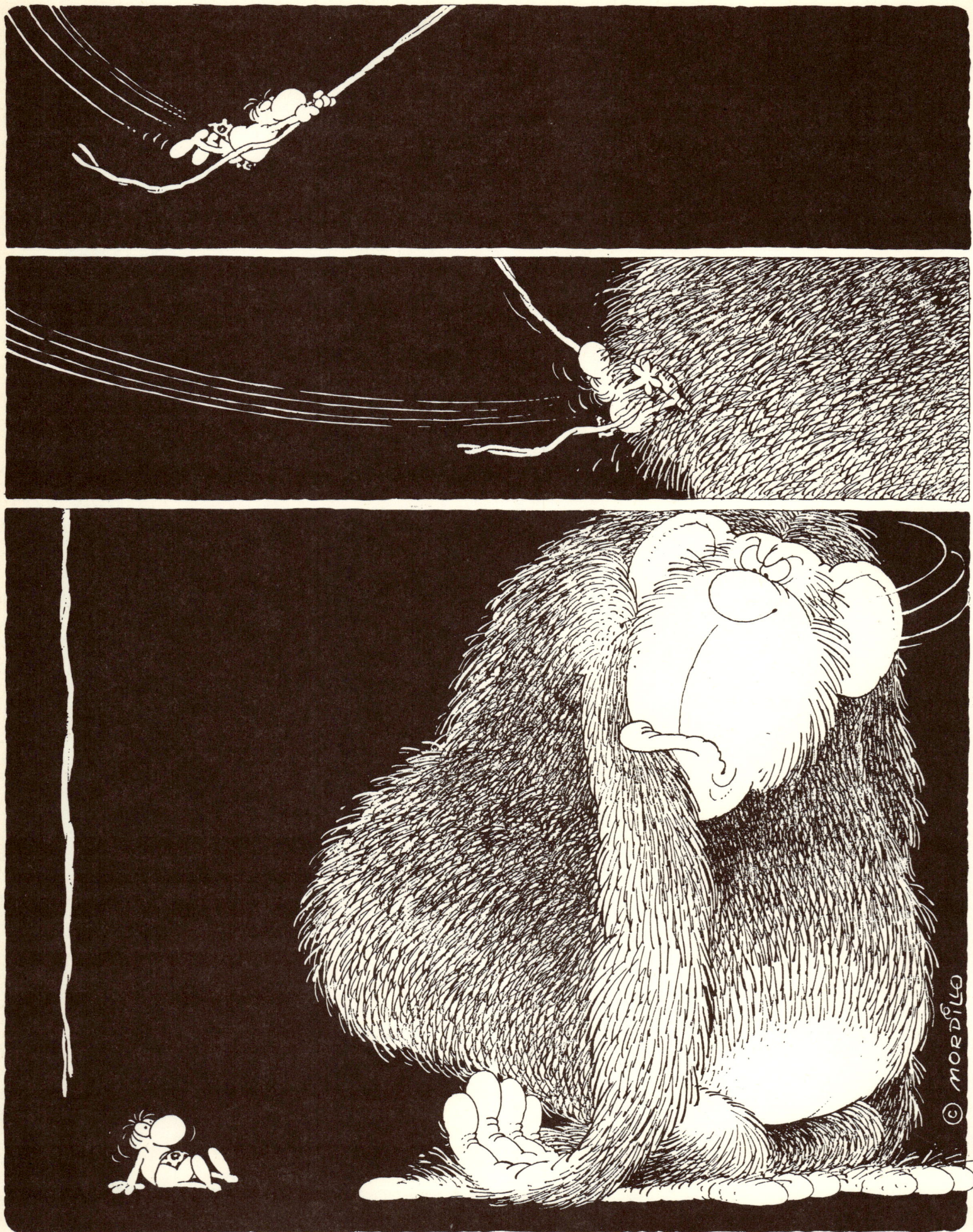

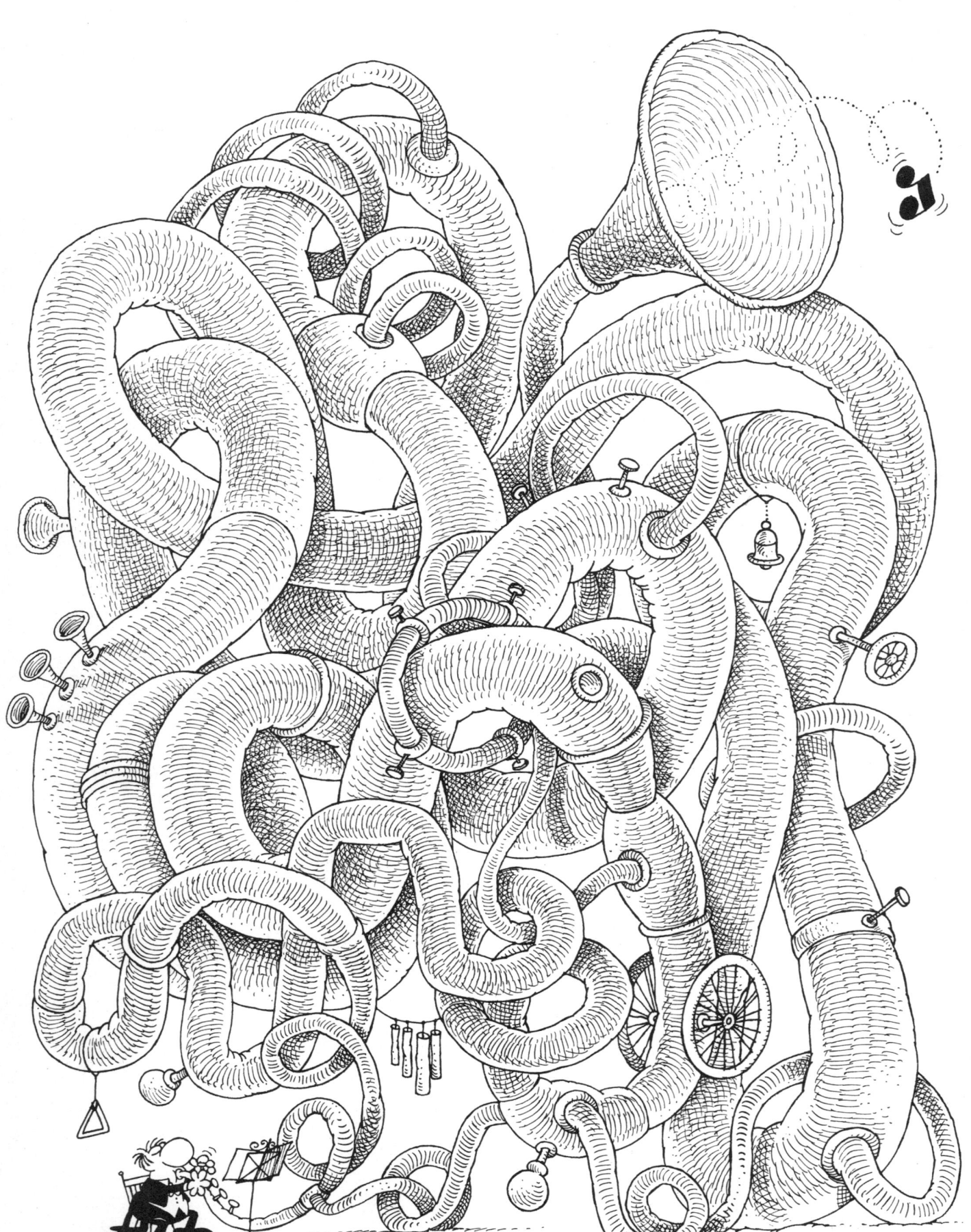

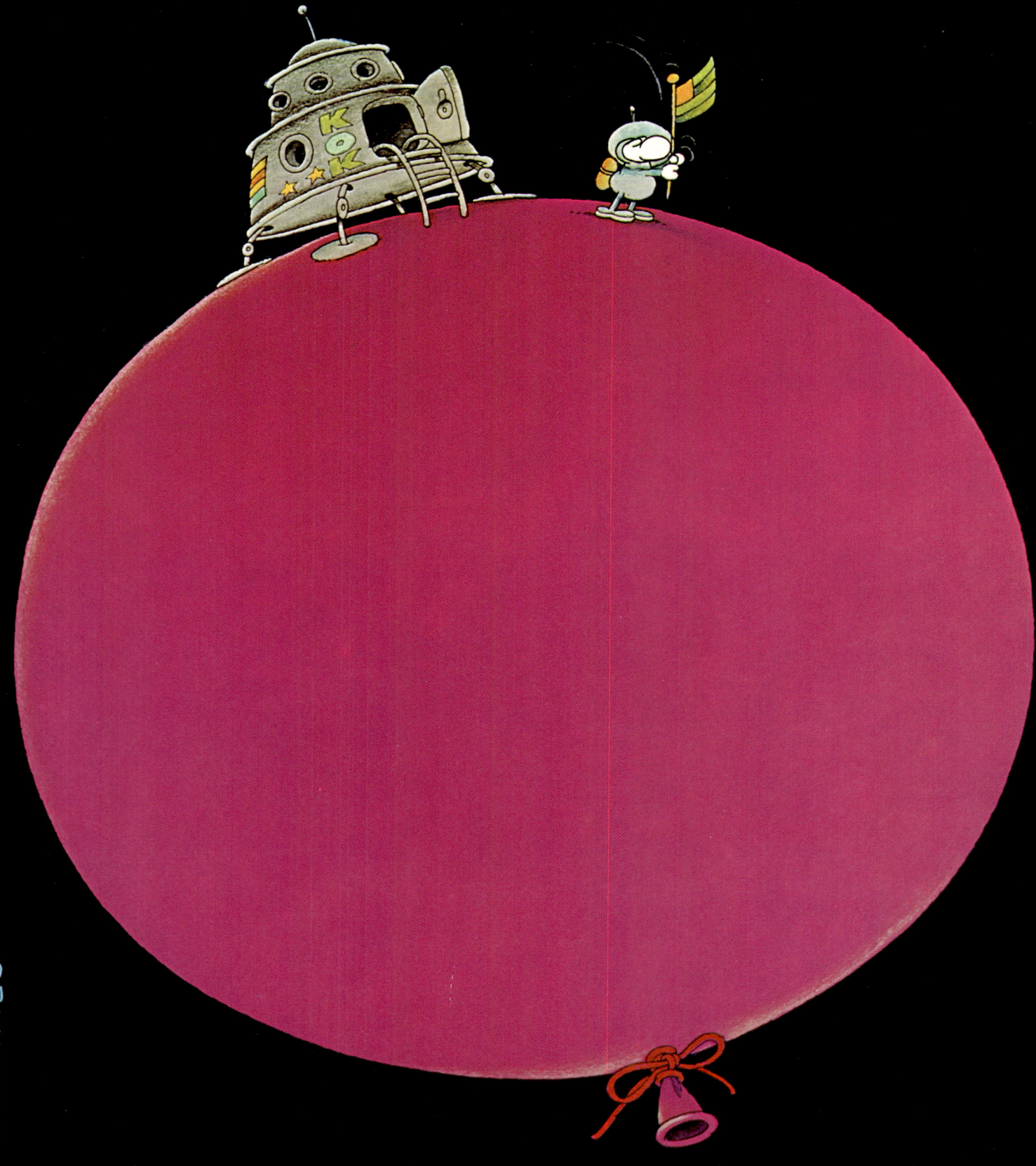

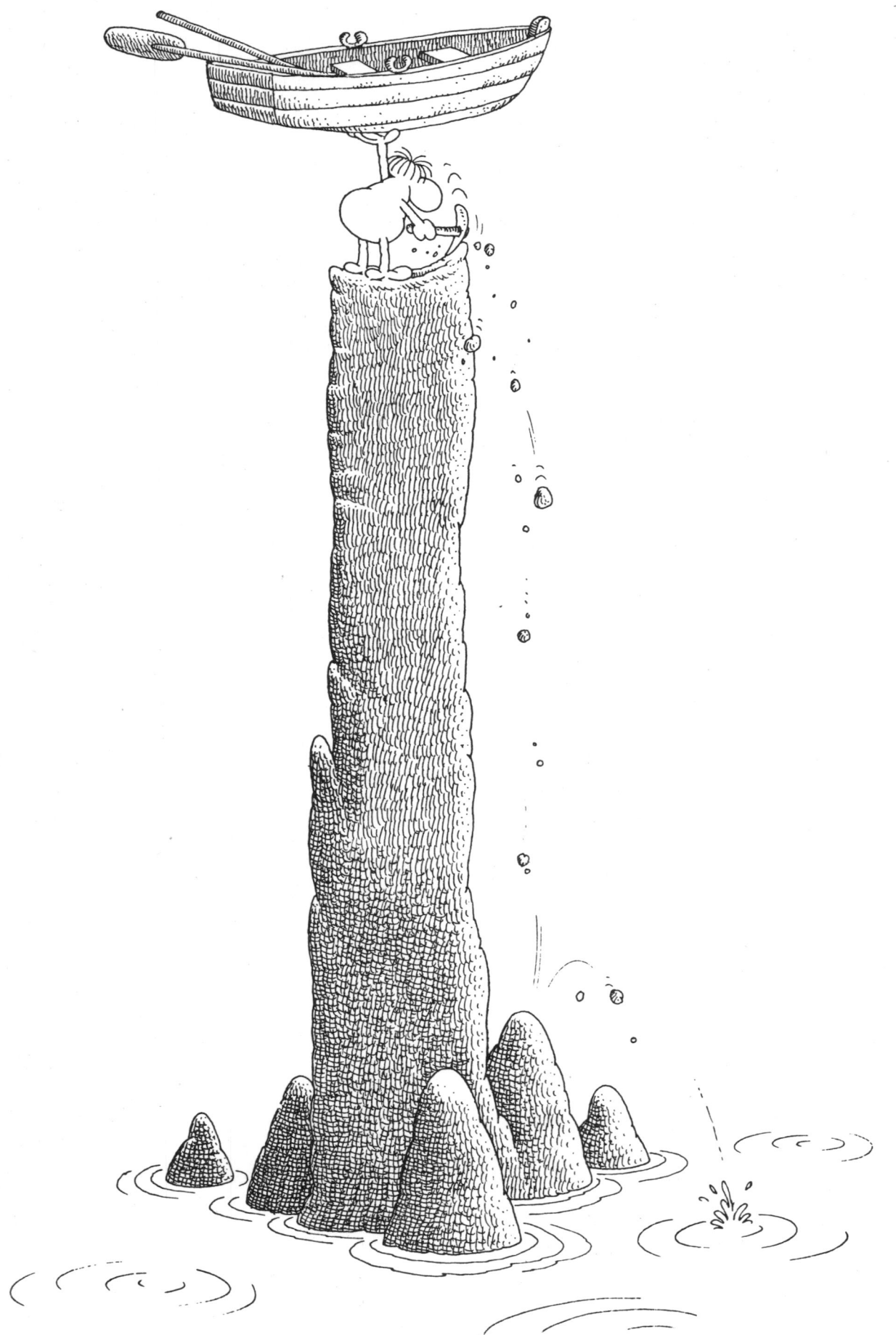

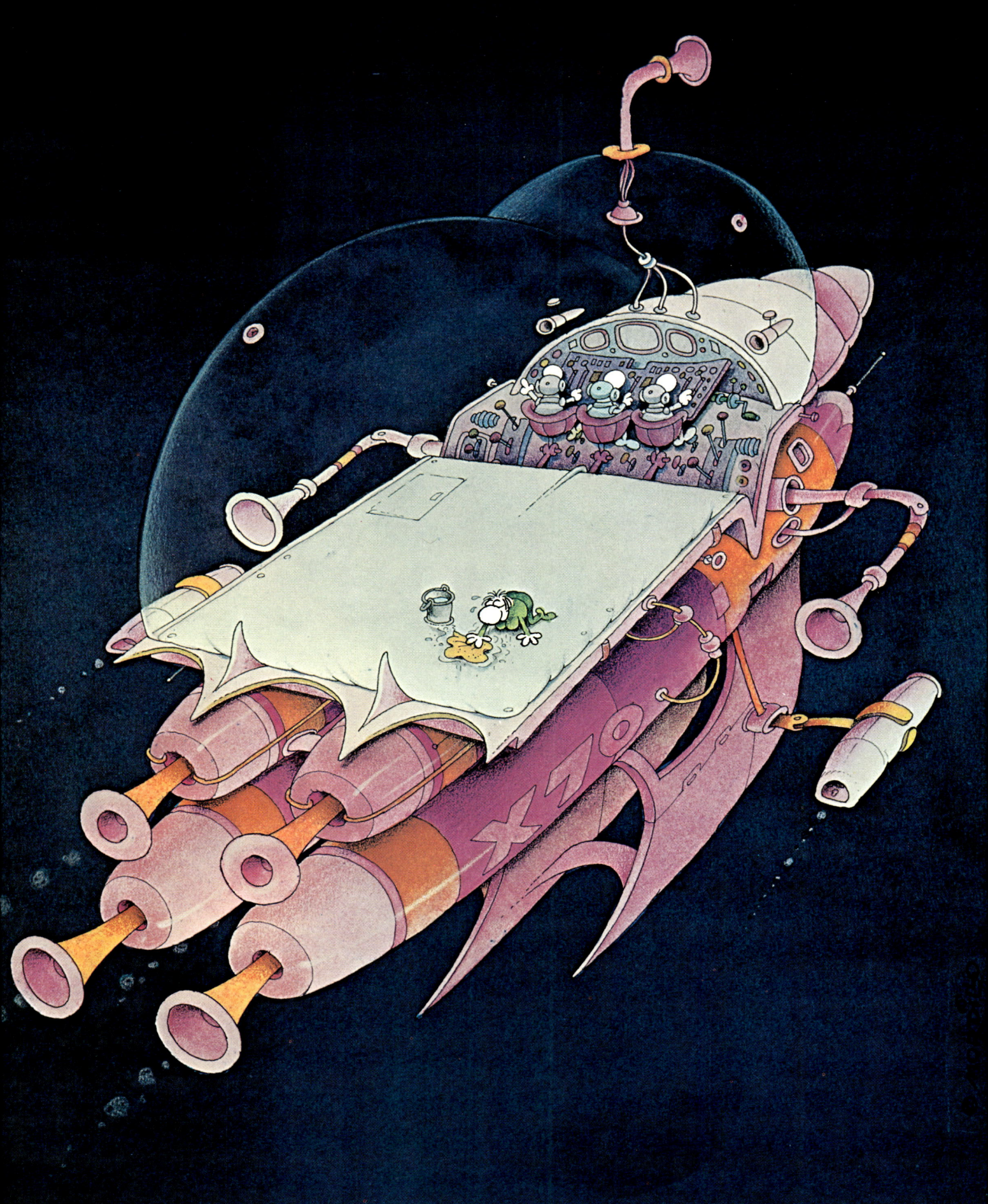

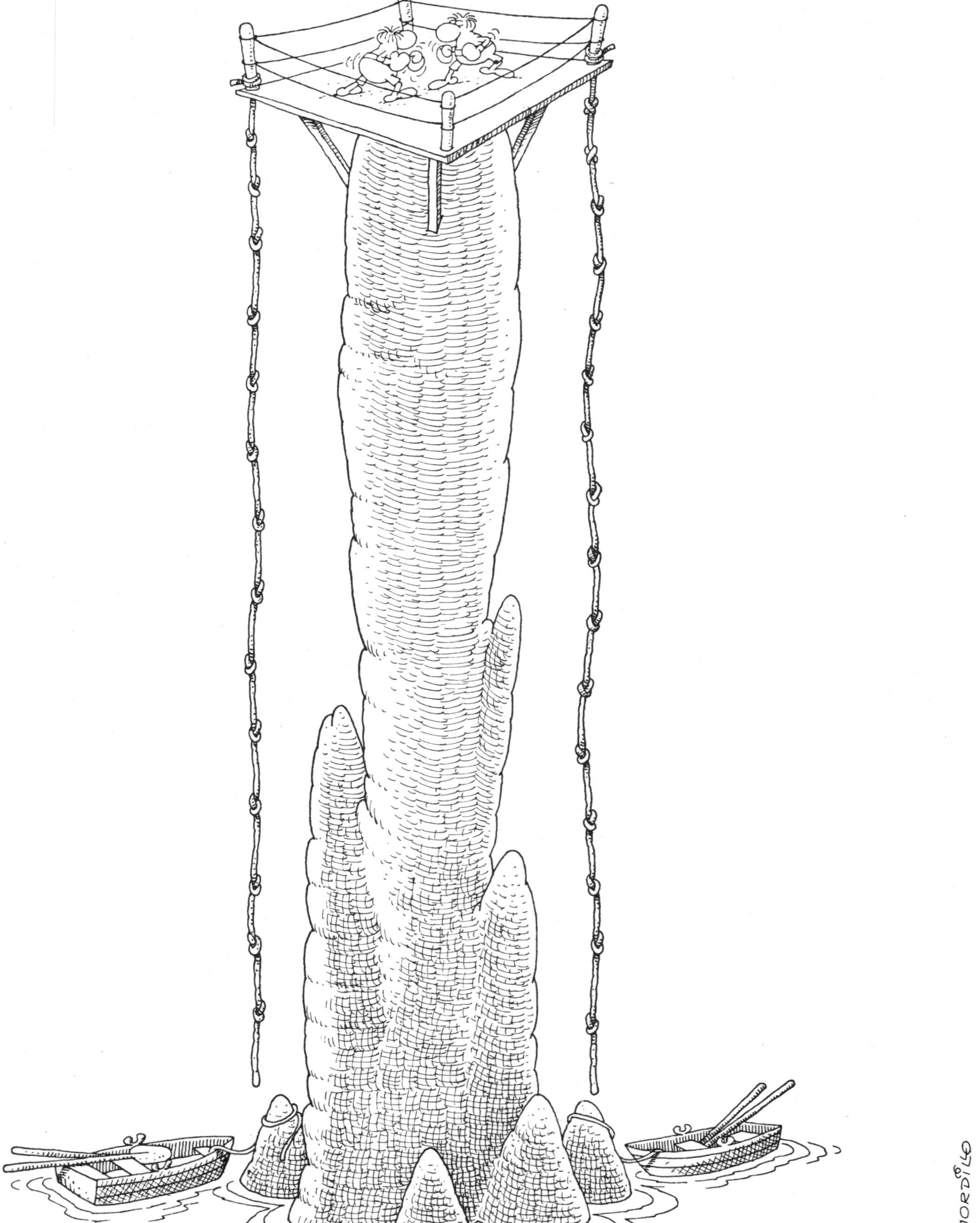
© MORDILLO

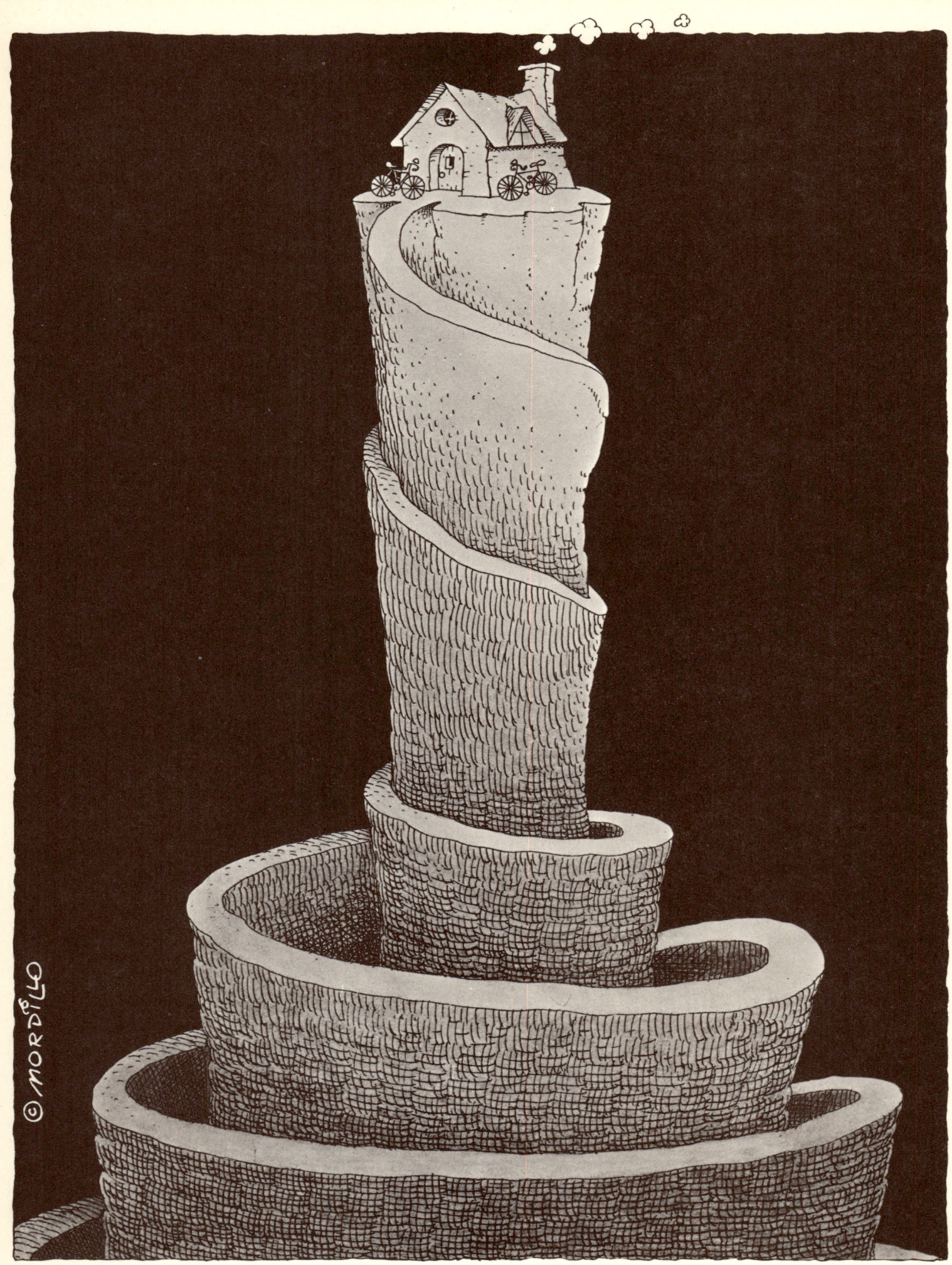

W

Also by Mordillo
Cartoons/Opus 1
Variations in colour and ink on the
theme of mankind and other atmospheric
phenomena